AWESOME FREESTYLE BMX

Tricks & Stunts

by Lori Polydoros

Reading Consultant:
Barbara J. Fox
Reading Specialist
North Carolina State University

Content Consultants:

Bart de Jong
Owner
European BMX Connection

Keith Mulligan
Editor In Chief
Ride BMX/Transworld Media

CAPSTONE PRESS
a capstone imprint

Blazers is published by Capstone Press,
151 Good Counsel Drive, P.O. Box 669, Mankato, Minnesota 56002.
www.capstonepub.com

Books published by Capstone Press are manufactured with paper
containing at least 10 percent post-consumer waste.

Library of Congress Cataloging-in-Publication Data
Polydoros, Lori, 1968–
  Awesome freestyle BMX tricks and stunts / by Lori Polydoros.
    p. cm.—(Blazers. Big air)
  Includes bibliographical references and index.
  Summary: "Describes extreme stunts and tricks performed by professional
freestyle BMX riders"—Provided by publisher.
  ISBN 978-1-4296-5411-1 (library binding)
  1. Bicycle motocross—Juvenile literature. I. Title.
  GV1049.3.P65 2011
  796.6'2—dc22   2010030049

Editorial Credits
Megan Peterson and Aaron Sautter, editors; Tracy Davies and Kyle Grenz, designers;
    Eric Manske, production specialist

Photo Credits
Corbis/Bo Bridges, 19, 22–23
Fat Tony, cover, 5, 7, 8–9, 11, 12, 15, 17, 20–21, 25, 29
Newscom/Icon SMI/MMD/Carleton Hall, 26

Artistic Effects
iStockphoto/Guillermo Perales, Jason Lugo, peter zelei

Printed in the United States of America in Stevens Point, Wisconsin.
092010   005934WZS11

TABLE OF CONTENTS

JUMP, TWIST, AND SPIN!

Professional **freestyle** BMX riders push the limits of their sport. They amaze fans with high-flying jumps, twists, and spins. Riders practice for years to perform their jaw-dropping tricks and stunts.

freestyle—a type of bicycle motocross (BMX) riding that focuses on tricks, stunts, and jumps

TOOTHPICK GRIND

BMXers **grind** their bikes on handrails, ledges, and ramps. In a Toothpick Grind, the rider slides one of the front **pegs** across a handrail. The back tire stays up in the air.

grind—to slide the pegs of a bike across an object

pegs

peg—a part attached to a bike's axles used for a variety of freestyle BMX tricks

WALL RIDE

In BMX, a wall isn't just a wall. It's also a surface to ride on! BMXers pedal hard to gain enough speed to stick to walls. They ride until gravity pulls them down.

TUCK -NO- HANDER

Look! No hands! In a Tuck-No-Hander, the rider throws his arms out to his sides. His arms look like wings as he soars through the air. In a flash, the rider grabs the handlebars again.

NO-FOOTED CAN-CAN

To begin a No-Footed Can-Can, the rider rockets off the ramp. He flings his legs off to one side. The rider looks like he is about to jump off the bike!

TRUCKDRIVER

Riding with spinning handlebars? It's easier said than done. In a Truckdriver, the rider flies into a **360**. He spins the handlebars one, two, or three times before landing.

FACT: The top pro freestyle BMX riders compete at the X Games each year. This event also features other extreme sports like snowboarding and skateboarding.

360—a spin that is equal to a full circle, or 360 degrees

FLAIR

Can you imagine flipping and spinning all at once? Check out this Flair. The BMXer launches into a backflip. Halfway through the flip, the rider spins the bike in a half circle.

TAILWHIP BACKFLIP

Don't blink! The **Tailwhip** Backflip is over in a flash. In mid-backflip, the rider kicks the back of the bike. He pulls up his feet. The bike's frame spins in a circle as the rider completes the backflip.

FACT: In 1988 Joe Johnson became the first rider to pull off a single Tailwhip in the air.

tailwhip—a trick in which a rider whips the bike's frame around in a circle while keeping the handlebars and his or her body still

19

SUPERMAN SEAT GRAB

The Superman Seat Grab turns an ordinary BMXer into a superhero. The rider flies through the air and grabs the seat with one hand. Then he kicks his legs straight out behind him.

360 NO-HANDED BACKFLIP

The 360 No-Handed Backflip is a rare trick. The BMXer flies into the air and lets go of the handlebars. Then he pulls a backflip and spins a 360 at the same time.

FACT:
BMX rider Dave Mirra (right) has won more gold medals than any other X Games athlete.

720 & 900

BMXers seem to float high above **half-pipes**. In a 720, riders spin two 360s before landing. Some riders can pull off a 900. They spin around two-and-a-half times!

FACT: At the 2002 X Games, Mat Hoffman pulled off a No-Handed 900. He became the first rider to land this trick in competition.

half-pipe—a U-shaped ramp with high walls

BACKFLIP LOOKBACK

In a Backflip Lookback, a BMXer looks like a pretzel. Riders crank the handlebars and look backward while upside down. Then they swing the back of the bike forward with their legs.

FACT:
Some BMX riders learn new tricks by practicing over foam pits. The foam pits help keep riders safe from injuries.

DOWNSIDE TAILWHIP

The Downside Tailwhip is a dizzying trick. The rider flies up the ramp and spins in a half circle. At the same time, he whips the bike's frame around in the opposite direction!

GLOSSARY

360 (THREE SIKS-tee)—a spin that is equal to a full circle, or 360 degrees

freestyle (FREE-stile)—a type of bicycle motocross (BMX) riding that focuses on tricks, stunts, and jumps

grind (GRINDE)—to slide the pegs of a bike across an object

half-pipe (HAF-pipe)—a U-shaped ramp with high walls

peg (PEG)—a part attached to a bike's axles used for a variety of freestyle BMX tricks

tailwhip (TAYL-wip)—a trick in which the rider whips the bike's frame around in a circle while keeping the handlebars and his or her body still

READ MORE

McClellan, Ray. *BMX Freestyle*. Torque: Action Sports. Minneapolis: Bellwether Media, 2008.

Miller, Connie Colwell. *BMX Park*. X Games. Mankato, Minn.: Capstone Press, 2008.

Sandler, Michael. *Daring BMXers*. X-Moves. New York: Bearport Pub., 2010.

INTERNET SITES

FactHound offers a safe, fun way to find Internet sites related to this book. All of the sites on FactHound have been researched by our staff.

Here's all you do:

Visit *www.facthound.com*

Type in this code: 9781429654111

Check out projects, games and lots more at
www.capstonekids.com

INDEX